The Four-Themed Precious Garland

The Four-Themed Precious Garland

An Introduction to Dzogchen, the Great Completeness
(chos-bzhi rin-chen phreng-ba)

by

Longchen Rabjampa Drime Wözer
with oral commentary by
His Holiness Dudjom Rinpoche
and
Beru Khyentze Rinpoche
Translated, edited and prepared by
Alexander Berzin
in conjunction with
Sharpa Tulku
Matthew Kapstein

LIBRARY OF TIBETAN WORKS AND ARCHIVES

First Published, 1979.

Reprint 1985
Reprint 1993

ISBN: 81-85102-40-6

Published by the Library of Tibetan Works and Archives, Dharamsala, and printed at Indraprastha Press (CBT), 4 Bahadurshah Zafar Marg, New Delhi

Contents

Foreword

Once again, the Library of Tibetan Works and Archives introduces another publication in pursuit of its aim of cultural synthesis and preservation. The publication of Longchen Rabjampa Drime Wözer's *The Four-Themed Precious Garland* not merely lays open one of the great traditions of Tibet to the West, but is also an indication that the links with these traditions are being maintained through the recording of ancient literary achievements in English.

Dr. Alexander Berzin, the translator and editor of this ancient treatise, in conjunction with Sharpa Tulku and Matthew Kapstein, are to be thanked for rendering their work with a precision which is noteworthy.

May, 1979

Gyatsho Tshering
Director, LTWA

Introduction

In June 1975, His Holiness the Fourteenth Dalai Lama, as part of his programme to preserve and transmit the many lineages of Buddhism in Tibet, commissioned the Library of Tibetan Works and Archives to translate and prepare representative works from each of the major Tibetan Buddhist traditions. As a sample of the Nyingma style of teaching, and in particular of the Dzogchen (*rdzogs-chen*) or "Great Completeness" tradition, *The Four- Themed Precious Garland* (*chos-bzhi rin-chen phreng-ba*) by Longchen Rabjampa Drime Wözer (klong-chen rab-'byams-pa dri-med 'od-zer) was chosen, as published in *Miscellaneous Writings (Gsung thor bu) of Kun-mkhyen Klong-chen-pa Dri-med-'od-zer*, vol. 1, (Delhi, Sanje Dorje, 1973), folios 248-264.

Longchen Rabjampa (1308-1363,) along with Sakya Pandita and Je Tsongkhapa, are commonly recognized as the three main manifestations of Manjushri to have taught in Central Tibet. In his youth, Longchenpa received not only the Nyingma transmissions as passed down in his family, but studied as well with many of the great teachers of his day without regard to sect. Thus he received the combined Kadam and Sakya teachings of the Sutra Vehicle through his main Sakya Guru, Palden Lama Dampa Sonam Gyaltsen (dpal-ldan bla-ma dam-pa bsod-nams rgyal-mtshan), in addition to the corpus of both old and new translation tantras. Together with the Third Karmapa Rangjung Dorje, he studied under Rigdzin Kumararaja. Through the efforts of these three, the diverse streams of the "Innermost Essence (*snying-thig*)" teachings of Dzogchen were brought together and codified into one of the common grounds between the Nyingma and Karma Kagyu Traditions.

Longchenpa composed a vast number of synthetic treatises, the most noteworthy being his "Seven Treasuries (*mdzod-bdun*)," which are formulations of the Nyingma path, integrating the Sutra Vehicle with the tantras of Dzogchen. As a teacher, he travelled widely and during a long stay in what is now Bhutan, established Buddhism among the inhabitants of that region.

The Four-Themed Precious Garland is an elaboration of the Four Themes of Gampopa (*dag-po chos-bzhi*)", which this Kagyu Master had condensed from the Mahamudra and Kadam teachings. The four themes are (1) turning the mind to the Dharma, (2) practicing the Dharma as a path, (3) removing confusion while on the path and (4) purifying confusion into pristine awareness. These are accomplished through abandoning respectively attachment and grasping to (1) this life, (2) cyclic existence or samsara, (3) one's own welfare and (4) true inherent existence. This is their usual explanation and it is a common preliminary prayer among the Kagyu practitioners to request the Gurus for inspiration to accomplish these four. Here, Longchenpa expounds on these themes in terms of the Dzogchen teachings in the characteristically Nyingma style of explaining a graded path of nine Buddhist vehicles.

The preliminary work for this translation, particularly for the first two chapters, was done in Dharamsala, India, with Sharpa Tulku in consultation with Khetsun Sangpo Rinpoche. Background material was also provided by Lama Thubten Yeshe. The oral transmission of the text was received in New York in June 1976 from His Holiness Dudjom Rinpoche, the Supreme Head of the Nyingma Tradition. His Holiness Dudjom Rinpoche kindly consented to provide the oral commentary to the particularly difficult third chapter and to answer questions concerning other points in the text. The material was translated with Matthew Kapstein and appears in an indented format interspersed with the root text. The oral commentary to the fourth chapter was given in Bodh Gaya, India, in January 1977 by Beru Khyentze Rinpoche in consultation with the Nyingma Master Khenpo Thupten Mawa. Beru Khyentze Rinpoche, also known as the Third Jamyang Kyentse Wangpo Rinpoche is a Lama of the Karma Kagyu Tradition who is also well-versed in the Nyingma Dzogchen teachings which he studied with the late Kunu Lama Rinpoche Tenzin Gyaltsen.

The original Tibetan for the technical terms used in this translation may be found in *Tibetan-English Dictionary of Buddhist Terminology* to be published shortly also by the Library of Tibetan Works and Archives.

It is hoped that this work will be of some small benefit to those who read it.

April, 1977

Alexander Berzin
Dharamsala, India

The Four-Themed Precious Garland

Sanskrit: Dharmacatur-ratnamala

Tibetan: Chos-bZhi Rin-po-che'i Phreng-wa

by

Longchen Rabjampa

Prologue

Homage to all the Buddhas and Bodhisattvas.

With supreme hundred-fold faith I make offerings to you, O sun-like Buddhas. Your nature is the sky-like expanse of your Body that Subsumes Everything (Dharmakaya). In it the (solar) mandala of your Form Body having five certainties[1] bursts forth and causes lotus-like disciples to bloom by the rays of your deeds.

The cool shade of the precious wish-granting tree of the ways of the Victorious One's teachings (of the Dharma) offers protection from all the torments of samsaric life and complacent liberation. I shall therefore explain this massive tree of good qualities in four points as the way for all those with faith to enter step by step (into its shade). Listen well.

1 *Turning Your Mind to the Dharma*

Whoever wishes to cross the boundless ocean of cyclic existence must first of all think to make an effort in this lifetime now to achieve the peace and happiness which is the phenomenon of liberation. A human body, difficult to obtain and easily lost, is a raft of liberties and endowments (for Dharma study and practice). Having attained one, if you do not exert yourself (to take advantage of it), you will never be free from the ocean of samsaric life. You will never stop its flow of (lifetimes filled with) many various sufferings. You will be tossed about in this unbearable, fearsome great ocean (of samsara) where the tides of delusions extend to the highest realm, the foam of sickness and old age is splashed everywhere and no end to the current of birth and death can be seen.

But whoever hears the teachings will be able to stop the flow of birth and death and will never be parted from supreme great bliss. Therefore with the excellent and precious raft of the supreme Dharma (which brings) peace, make an effort to cross the ocean of the three realms' delusions.

If you do not practice the enlightening path to liberation now, in the future you will never even hear the name "fortunate rebirth." Through endless unfortunate lifetimes, one after the other, you will have no method for becoming free from cyclic existence. Therefore, now that you have attained a human body of liberty and endowments, those of you with sense should practice sincerely and with great effort. That will bring you benefit and bliss. By means of this, you will be able to accomplish the aims of both yourself and others.

Even if you have attained the liberties and endowments, there is never any mental security. Everything is insecure, changes and has no essence. As all things are momentary, impermanent and disintegrate, you should think from your heart about how you will quickly die.

It is the same with the entire world all around you. It too will disintegrate by (the forces of) the seven fires, one flood and wind.[2] Not even a single tip of a hair will remain. Everything will become empty; there will be only space. Those who live in it—impermanent fleeting beings, that is gods, anti-gods, humans, animals, hungry ghosts and hell creatures—whatever sentient beings there are, when their time is up, must plunge into the waters of death, transference of consciousness and rebirth. Years, months, days and divisions of time are momentary, impermanent, they disintegrate and are (continually) passing. As there are such sad things as the changing of the four seasons, think about how your own life as well will be impermanent.

There is no mental security whatsoever. Very soon life will depart from your body. Therefore from today on you must definitely think, "It is completely uncertain which will happen first, tomorrow or the time when my life span shall be spent."

The suffering of birth is more fearsome than that of death. There is never any happiness no matter where you are born, for the nature of cyclic existence is like that of a blazing fire. Therefore seek a method for becoming liberated from it right now.

Hell creatures are tormented by heat and cold, hungry ghosts by hunger and thirst, animals by the devouring of each other, stupidity and ignorance and human beings by the three and eight faults.[3] Anti-gods (suffer from) fighting and war, gods from death, transference of consciousness and falling (to lower rebirths). Their happiness can change into grief and their suffering of extensiveness is great. After their consciousness is transferred from the pleasures and comfort of the god realms, they may enter the fires of a hell once again. Thinking in this way, work to go beyond samsaric existence.

The appearances of this life are just like a dream before you are about to wake up. They are changing and impermanent. Because you must go leaving them behind, what can retinue, wealth and so forth do for you? Make an effort in the Dharma right now.

Desire is like poison, weapons or fire. (Once it strikes) its torment is constant and so there is never a chance for happiness. (What is entailed is) the suffering of working to gather, protect and increase (what you desire and consequently) you are always bound by hoarding, stinginess and greed. Fighting with everyone, your defiled delusions increase. Your mind wanders with busy-work and it threatens your body and life.

Having too many involvements and activities contradicts your Dharma practice and is always despised by the Noble Ones, the Aryas. If your desires are few, your virtuous actions will increase automatically. Therefore you who wish to engage yourselves on the path to peaceful liberation, lessen your desires and be content.

It is said that if you exhaust your desires, you are a real Arya and if your desires are few, you are nearly an Arya. Just as suffering and delusions increase for those with desire, virtuous actions increase for those with little desire. Therefore follow in the footsteps of the holy masters of the past. Be always content and have few possessions.

The faults of being with people are really limitless. There is far too much useless distraction and activities. Anger, arguments and fighting increase, and attraction and repulsion arise. You always become infected with their bad habits and this is pointless. No matter what you do, there is never a time when you can really please them. No matter how much you try to show them, the chances are slim to benefit them. No matter how much you listen to them, nothing good ever comes of it. No matter how close you are to someone, like your best friend, in the end you will have to part. Therefore abandon all involvements in which you are dependent on followers, friends or relatives. Make a definite effort from today on to live in quiet solitude in order to practice the pure Dharma.

Supreme holy beings of the past have said that living in quietude they found the nectar (of Dharma experience). Therefore resolve that you too shall live alone in a secluded forest in order to attain (a state of) peace.

Living in quietude has been praised by the Victorious Buddhas. With no one to annoy you, deep single-minded concentration increase. You naturally practice the Dharma and somber thoughts of impermanence arise. Your possessions are put aside and you have no busy-work or distractions. Masses of good qualities like faith and renunciation multiply and, because there is no involvement with people, your activities automatically become fewer.

Therefore, without the eight worldly feelings,[4] not worrying about making other happy or about saving face, pass your days and nights with the Dharma in the bliss of having total freedom. (In this way) make your attainment of a fully endowed body of liberty and endowments meaningful and take full advantage of it. As the benefits of all this are inexpressible, try to practice deep concentration for your entire life in complete solitude alone in a forest.

May the cooling rain of the Dharma, well explained in this way, extinguish the thought that is afflicted by delusion. May it fill the lotus pond of the collection of virtues of single-minded concentration. May it expand the attainment of the Land of Peace.

2 *Practicing the Dharma as a Path*

Suppose that on faith you have entered the supreme, holy and virtuous Dharma and you now wish further to be on a path to liberation. (What you must do is actually) put the Dharma into practice as a path (that is as a way of life). This is essential in order to tame your mind.

There are those who have entered the teachings of the Victorious Buddhas in this way and have even embarked upon a course of hearing, thinking about and meditating (on the teachings). Yet some are not tranquil: they have base minds. Some pursue incorrect or inferior paths or ones that lead astray. Some have great desires and craving, and some are distracted with concerns for this life. All such mistakes, contradictory to the Dharma, arise from not practicing the Dharma as a path. The faults that come from this in this and future lives are measureless. Whoever is fooled by such deceptions will have regret at the time of death and will have terror and anxiety in the in-between (*bar-do*) period. He will go to a lower rebirth state in the future and never have the opportunity to be permanently liberated from cyclic existence. Therefore practice the Dharma as a path.

Although people take hygienic medicine to cure their sickness, if they do not take it properly, they may become sicker than before. Likewise, what use is the Dharma if it is not followed properly as a cure. Therefore, as there are limitless faults like this, those of you with faith should understand this well.

Concerning this, practicing the Dharma as a path depends, first of all, on your spiritual master. Therefore it is important to rely on a holy, fully qualified guru. Whatever good qualities there are come from this.

As for him, he should be someone with compassion and skilful means, who is tranquil, has self-control and is patient. His vows, words of honor and mode of behavior should be excellent and complete. He should have heard many (teachings) and practiced them well. His waves of inspiration should be measureless, automatically influencing the appearance of others. He should be unconcerned with this life and cleansed like the sky of the eight worldly feelings. Such a person, who makes the life of anyone associated with him meaningful and places him on a path to liberation, is a form of the Victorious Ones manifested at the time of the deteriorations. Therefore devote yourself (to him) perfectly with great respect.

The benefits from this are measureless and inexhaustible. You become disgusted with samsaric existence and renounce it. Thus your thoughts for this life lessen. In your mind you let go (concern) for this life and your grasping for true identities based on deceptive appearances falls apart. You will naturally have self-control and will listen to, think about and meditate on (the teachings). You will acquire many extensive good qualities such as faith. Your present life will become meaningful and your future ones will reap the results. Therefore devote yourself to a holy (master).

Moreover, you should never be dishonest with the three gates (of your body, speech and mind). Be like a patient to his doctor, a merchant (travelling on the sea) to his navigator, a passenger to his oarsman, a guest to his escort. Try always to please him with respectful service. It is taught that if you develop a disrespectful (attitude) or distorted view (of him), you enter a hellish rebirth for (as many eons as) the number of moments (you develop it). Therefore protect, as you would your eyes, your various words of honor (to respect him). Do this by confessing (if you ever violate them), restraining yourself and feeling great regret (should you ever break them).

Devote yourself in this way to a supreme spiritual master and cultivate your mind-stream by listening to, thinking about and meditating on (his teachings). Then intentionally transform whatever you do into virtue with the thought of desiring only liberation. This is an oral tradition teaching of how to practice the Dharma as a path.

Whenever you listen (to the teachings), think about or recite them, undertake these for the sake of liberating your mind-stream. Whenever you write, read, memorize or teach, pursue these desiring only liberation. In your meditation, philosophizing and conduct, too, try strongly to feel renunciation and disgust with samsara by never separating your mind from being set only on liberation. There is nothing higher than these essential oral teachings.

Eating, sleeping, walking, sitting, talking, speaking, thinking and so forth-in short, whatever activities you do, never let your mind stray from the wish for liberation. Develop disgust (with samsara) and thus tame your mind-stream. This is the essential point for practicing the Dharma as a path.

Furthermore, to travel the Mahayana path in particular, you should direct whatever virtuous actions you do towards the sake of others. Thus in order to benefit sentient beings, you should whole-heartedly practice developing a compassionate enlightened motive of bodhichitta, having fervent regard (for enlightenment and helping others), dedicating (your merit) and rejoicing (in your own and others' virtues). In this connection (you should recognize that in previous lives) all beings have been your mother and father, relatives and dear friends. Thus it is fitting that they receive your help.

Your yourself must develop an enlightened motive for the sake of others. Then practice virtue for the benefit of all beings. By your virtuous actions, others will become happy. You should cultivate and enhance your enlightened motive with immeasurable compassion by thinking, "May everyone's suffering ripen on me and my virtuous actions ripen on them. May all beings attain Buddhahood."

Whatever virtuous actions you do, precede them with developing an enlightened motive, carry them out without objectifying anything and conclude them by dedicating the merit. Moreover, you should completely purify (yourself of misconceptions about the true nature of) the three spheres—the object of what is to be practiced, what is being practiced and the one who is practicing. Like illusions, they are mere appearances (based) on nothing real, like magical creations. Therefore purifying the natures (of these three), you should dedicate the merit in order to benefit others.

Fervent regard is having extreme faith in the Victorious Buddhas, their Dharma teachings, their holy (Bodhisattva) offsprings and in the objects for accumulating merit—in all these, without exception. From having regard for benefiting yourself, others and both (yourself and others) you will receive praise, respect and esteem beyond all examples.

Rejoicing is meditating on happiness over all the virtuous acts of the Buddhas, Bodhisattva offsprings and all beings. This is a supreme method for transforming limitless masses of merit into great immeasurable (pristine awareness).

Pure prayers should be offered in order to benefit beings. In this connection the oral tradition teaching of purifying the objects of your practice should be meditated upon.

> Whatever action you do should be accompanied with a purifying prayer. For instance, when walking you should pray that all beings likewise proceed to the state of enlightenment; when eating, that everyone be able to live on the nourishment of single-minded concentration; when inhaling, that you clear away and dissolve all the delusions of those about you; when exhaling, that you give others bliss; and so forth.

Never be distracted for even a moment to ordinary

things. Take as your essential practice working for others and doing virtue with the three gates (of your body, speech and mind). Taming your mind-stream so as to have an outstanding development of an enlightened motive is said to be the way to make any practice of Dharma into a path (to enlightenment).

In this way may the melodious beat of the sound of the drum of the profound meaning, the well-known sweet boom which is both vast and profound, wake all beings from the intoxication and sleep of their ignorance. May they see extensively a joyous festival of peace.

3 *Removing Confusion While on the Path*

Furthermore, there are common, special and peerless methods for removing confusion while on the path.

> When travelling the path to be taken after turning your mind to the Dharma, it is essential to remove all confusion and possible sources of error. Otherwise there will be many obstacles and hindrances.

The first of these is the great Mahayana path (of the sutras) which is followed in common (by all Mahayana traditions). On it you cultivate an enlightened motive of bodhichitta (on the basis of) the four immeasurables.[5] Endowed thus with prayer and compassion, you eliminate confusion (that might impede your progress) by working exuberantly (for others). With (bodhichitta having) the nature of voidness and compassion, you will be able to fulfil completely the purpose of yourself and others.

> There are two levels of bodhichitta, relative and ultimate. The former is the motive to attain enlightenment in order to be able to liberate all beings and is developed through compassion. The latter is the realization of the true nature of reality and is cultivated through voidness meditation. With their joint attainment, which is of means and wisdom, you achieve Buddhahood and the ability to fulfil the aims of everyone to be free from suffering.

In order to cleanse away fleeting stains from the void sphere of all things, which is virtuous and unconditioned, you must meditate on the thirty-seven facets of the path to perfection while on the paths of accumulation, preparation, seeing and meditation.[6]

> In Buddhahood you fully realize your Buddha-nature, which is synonymous with the void sphere of all things (dharmadhatu), the substratum of everything, the unconditioned abiding nature of reality. Your Buddha-nature, however, is obscured by the fleeting stains of ignorance, confusion, the moral and mental defilements and so forth. To cleanse it, therefore, you must pass through four paths of stages on which you practice thirty-seven facets that bring about your attainment of perfection.

(In addition) you must fully realize the pure, correct view of the sixteen types of voidness[7] and complete the faultless practice of the six perfections.[8] And (in particular for the perfection of wisdom) you must understand the identitylessness of both the conventional "I" and all phenomena. Using these methods as an antidote, you cleanse yourself of the moral and mental defilements. This is the excellent path of the Bodhisattvas.

> This path can be further elaborated as follows.

Although everything exists (on the conventional level) only in the manner of mirages, dreams and deceptive appearances, you abandon and adopt (appropriate practice on the paths to enlightenment), work for the sake of others, avoid (non-virtuous actions) and undertake (virtuous ones) You cleanse away the defilements of longing desire, fearful and angered repulsion and closed-mindedness with the waters of (their antidotes, namely meditation on) ugliness, love and interdependent origination.

Concerning the two levels of truth, in relative or operative reality all things are like mirages or dreams. Based on these, however, you practice and work to benefit others through the six perfections and other methods mentioned in the Mahayana scriptures. You apply direct opponents to your delusions by meditating on their opposites. For instance, to dampen longing desire you meditate on the ugliness and imperfection of what you long to posses. You develop love for that which you hate and break through closed-mindedness by studying the intricate mechanism of interdependent origination. Through such methods you can overcome and remove the confusion of the defilements obscuring your Buddha-nature and thus the path to your realization of enlightenment will become clear and open.

Because the ultimate level of truth is unborn and pure, it is without such dualistic (distinctions) as samsara and nirvana. It is free from such mental fabrications (of the conventional mind).

To cultivate ultimate bodhichitta, you must realize that the ultimate, abiding nature of reality is not something born from causes and circumstances. It is perfectly pure and free from mental fabrications such as the divisions into samsara and nirvana, virtuous and non-virtuous, good and bad, and so forth.

When you have ascertained the meaning of the perfection of wisdom (prajnaparamita), which is the voidness of both the conventional "I" and all phenomena, there is no longer the two extremes of samsara and nirvana. Such divisions are the deceptive appearances of the relative level of truth. From the point of view of

> the ultimate level, then, there is only voidness. The unity of these two levels is the supreme view.

This is the meaning of the two truths. The path of interdependent origination is the causal Mahayana vehicle of philosophical studies.

> The appearance of all things of samsara and nirvana is based on the causal processes of interdependent origination. These appearances are undeniable. They are the unceasing natural play of voidness, like the play of light, the play of eddies and waves on the water and the rustling of the leaves. All things of relative reality are this way. Thus because appearances are irrefutable, there is the relative or operative level of truth.
>
> On the ultimate level there are no validly cognised objects other than the one taste of the absence of all mental fabrications. Ultimate reality transcends the division into subject and object. It is the underlying stratum, the unborn, pure mode of existence of the appearances of the relative level. Thus the two levels of truth are inseparable.
>
> As for ascertaining the meaning of voidness, both the Sutrayana approach and that of Dzogchen amount to exactly the same thing. The two systems may label and divide things differently, but no matter how they formulate it, the nature of voidness is the same. The distinctive feature here of the causal Mahayana vehicle is that as you cultivate your mind you become more and more learned through philosophical studies and thus increasingly broad in your outlook. It is known as "causal" because on it you practice as the path such causes for attain-

> ing Buddhahood as the six perfections, the thirty-seven facets of the path to perfection and variety of ethical and intellectual disciplines. Buddhahood emerges as the result when all such causes are complete.
>
> Developing the two types of bodhichitta, relative and ultimate, and ascertaining the meaning of the corresponding two levels of truth, then, are the instructions for removing confusion while on the path according to this common Mahayana vehicle of the sutras.

The special Mahayana path of the secret tantras has outer and inner (divisions). It has the fathomlessly supreme method of the unity of the development and completing stages by which you cleanse away confusion through various stages.

> Both the development and completing stages of tantra entail various practices for eliminating impure, deceptive cognition obscuring the path. The former involves complex visualizations and the latter meditation on voidness. It is insufficient to practise merely one of these stages by itself. The visualizations should not be taken as concrete; you must recognize that their foundation is voidness. Furthermore, voidness should not be taken nihilistically as denying everything. It does not impede interdependent origination. Thus the unity (yuganaddha) of the development and completing stages means their simultaneous practice—not doing one without the other.

In the three outer classes of tantras, the main emphasis is on purification. You abandon and adopt in turn (what is appropriate) and thus eliminate taints by (applying their) antidotes.

On the level of practice of the three outer tantras—kriya, charya and yoga—you are unable as yet to transform delusions or defilements into pristine awareness. Therefore you abandon the former and adopt the latter. You apply direct opponents or antidotes to the moral and mental defilements such as the purifying practices of ritual ablution and annointment, meditation on love and compassion, and so forth.

To practise these in turn means to apply whichever antidote is necessary in terms of whatever tainting defilement is absent or present in a given situation. Because the path is conceived in terms of defilements to be cleansed and opposing antidotes to cleanse them, there is this application in turn. These outer tantras are quite difficult to practise.

As for the inner (tantras), through pristine awareness which is an undivided unity, those things to be abandoned become the path through (the application of) means.

The inner tantras are those of maha-, anu- and ati-yoga. In their practice you realize pristine awareness (jnana, *ye-shes*), which is an undivided unity of method and wisdom—in other words the unity of relative and ultimate realities from the point of view of this unity's being a cognitive function. Through the totality of this pristine awareness those things to be abandoned, such as the defilements together with their suffering, are utilized, when then arise, as aspects of the path through the application of appropriate means. This does not mean that you encourage the arisal of defiled states of mind. Rather, there is no need for the deliberate action of "abandoning" delusions; they are automatically

> transcended with such awareness. This is the distinctive feature of the three higher tantras.

All things appear naturally on the mandala which is the foundation expanse, the Buddha-nature, and do so merely through your own mind.

> Ultimate reality is the mandala of the perfectly pure expanse of voidness. It is like a "magic" mirror. What unimpededly appears on it are all the things (dharmas) of relative reality, your mind included. These things appear naturally on this "magic" mirror, through and to your mind. There is no third reality of a truly existing mind or objects juxtaposed to the ultimate reality of the mirror and the relative reality of the images in it.

They are confusing deceptions and do not really exist. They are void forms which nevertheless appear distinctly as the aggregate physical and mental faculties, the cognitive bases and spheres and so forth. Regarded purely, they are the Buddha-families and so on.

> All phenomena of relative reality are void by nature. Deceptively they appear truly to exist, but do not really do so. Yet from voidness various distinct appearances do arise, for instance forms. They are reflections of the "magic" mirror, voidness, and appear distinctly as your aggregates and as the consciousness, cognitive power and objects of your mind and senses. With pure vision you experience them in a subtler manner. You regard your five aggregate faculties as the five "Dhyani" Buddhas, your five bodily elements (earth, water, fire, air and space) as the five consorts, your eight types of consciousness (foundation, defiled, mental and the five sensory) as the eight meditational

> Bodhisattvas and so forth. Thus your entire body and all your defilements are regarded as having a divine nature.

Thus on the development stage all that appears is united into a single mandala. Bodies become deities, speech becomes mantra, and memories and thoughts are applied to emanating and absorbing (pristine awareness. In this way) ordinary deceptive appearances are regarded as a Buddha-field.

> Relative things ordinarily appear to be concrete. This is deceptive because in actuality they lack true existence. When this confusing deception is transcended with pristine awareness, they are experienced in a wholly different, subtler manner. From the viewpoint of the unity of voidness and appearance, everything is in fact a perfect Buddha-field—a mandala filled with deities. There is nothing there that can still be referred to as a "deceptive appearance."
>
> All bodies and speech encountered become deities and mantras through this pure type of vision. Whatever thought or memories occur are viewed as the play of pristine awareness through visualizing such awareness in various forms emanating from you and then re-absorbing. This whole practice in which there is the necessity to transform body, speech and mind into deities, mantras and so forth in order to eliminate confusion about them is the path of the development stage.

Through (the procedures of) the completing stage, you enter the inconceivable sphere of clear light in which everything is in the state of its actual void nature. (This is accomplished) through the yoga methods dealing with the energy-channels, energy currents and creative energies. Your consciousness and energy-currents come under your control and become usable.

> On the completing stage of the inner tantras you treat your body as energy-channels (nadi), your speech as energy-currents (prana) and your mind as creative energy (bindu). While practicing the yoga methods concerning these energy-systems, you meditate on the nature of the mind as pristine awareness characterized by great bliss. As a result, these currents of energy become usable for achieving the ordinary and extraordinary powerful attainments (siddhi). There are many examples of Master Practitioners (Mahasiddha) of the past who have performed miraculous deeds because of their mastery of such methods. These may be known from historical accounts.

The sphere of voidness and pristine awareness become conjoined. The indivisible unity (which is their conjunction) is the path of Mahamudra. This is the resultant Vajrayana vehicle of the secret tantras.

> Through the above techniques you realize the unity of voidness and pristine awareness or, in other words, of voidness and its unimpeded play. Thus you attain a Buddha's Body of Pristine Awareness (Jnanakaya), the cognitive aspect of the Body of the Essential Nature (Svabhavakaya)—this latter one being the abiding nature of all reality. Because Buddhahood is understood to be identical with this abiding nature, there is no need to deal with the causes for its arisal. Rather, emphasis is placed on cultivating the realization of this reality. Thus the Mahamudra path of the tantras continually deals

with its result or aim, the state of Buddhahood, and therefore is referred to as the resultant path.

The yoga of the energy-channels and so forth is the foremost feature of anu-yoga. It is also practised in ati-yoga, just as ati- is in maha-yoga. In fact, all three inner tantras are mutually pervasive, incorporating aspects of one another. A certain practice is classified as maha-, anu- or ati-yoga in reference to what is emphasized or is foremost in it. The prominent feature of a maha-yoga practice is the development stage, that of anu-yoga is the completing stage, while that of ati-yoga or Dzogchen is the cultivation of the realization of the void sphere of all things. Each of these practices, however, has development (maha), completing (anu) and Dzogchen (ati) stages. For the purpose of theoretical exposition, it is easier to understand if these three inner tantras are treated separately.

For example, in a maha-yoga practice you begin with meditation on voidness, seeing everything purified into the void. From this state arise exuberant waves of the motivation of compassion. This is called "single-pointed concentration appearing everywhere." When the unity of voidness and compassion is established through such meditation, it is called "single-minded concentration on suchness."

In this state the arisal of pure awareness is practiced through meditation on a visualized seed syllable such as "HUM." Rays of light proceed from it, purifying the entire environment of samsara and the beings within it. All are realized to be of the nature of voidness. Through such a process the world becomes a Buddha-field or the divine realm of a meditational deity, buildings become the celestial palace of the deity and your mind becomes the seed syllable. If this syllable is HUM, then at the next stage it becomes a vajra or lightning-sceptre of the enlightened motive of bodhichitta. From this vajra, light proceeds and that in turn becomes the meditational deity, for instance Vajrasattva. Proceeding thus through many extensive stages you practice the development stage of maha-yoga tantra.

In an anu-yoga practice the above stages are somewhat abbreviated. Foremost emphasis is on the mastery of the yoga dealing with the energy-channels, energy-currents and creative energies.

Ati-yoga or Dzogchen is often known as "maha-ati," Here "maha" refers to the practice of a development stage as in maha-yoga. "Maha" literally means "great" and "ati" means "most." Realization of the abiding nature of reality is the highest or most supreme practice.

The reason why a maha-yoga development stage must be conjoined with an anu- or ati-yoga practice is as follows. If you have not meditated to at least a certain extent on visualizing Guru Rinpoche or some other deity and reciting his mantra, you will have nothing upon which to base your practice of an anu-yoga completing stage. You will lack a context within which to meditate upon the energy-system and voidness. Likewise if you have not trained yourself with a development stage practice of deliberately visualizing a deity and reciting a mantra, you will have no background or basis enabling you in ati-yoga to experience everything spontaneously as a perfect mandala, deity and so forth. Thus the three inner tantras are not practiced separately.

The supreme peerless vehicle of the secret Dzogchen, the Great Completeness, functions to bring you directly into the sphere of that which is spontaneously there. This sphere, which is the foundation, is unchanging. All good qualities (appear) in it spontaneously as the sun, moon, planets and stars do in the sky. It need not be sought for because it is spontaneously present from time immemorial. No trying or effort (is required). This path is naturally obvious.

> The foundational sphere or "founding stratum," which exists primordially, is identical with pure awareness. It never changes and is thus likened to the sky or space. In this space the various Buddha Bodies, qualities and pristine awareness arise spontaneously just as the sun, moon and so forth appear in the physical sky without being sought for. The planets and stars do not come about through your efforts, yet you see them. Likewise, without deliberate effort you can directly perceive the obvious path of voidness, because voidness by nature is directly perceivable. Dzogchen, then, is the path of voidness itself.

The mandala sphere of clear light is unconditioned. It is the innate Dharmakaya, the all-pervasive intentionality (of the Buddhas). To realize it directly is the supreme view of reality.

> The nature of voidness is clear light, which is pure and present from time immemorial. The mandala of that sphere of clear light is unconditioned by causes and circumstances. It is the innate Dharmakaya, the unconditioned abiding nature of all things, inherent in the mind-streams of all sentient beings. Thus the foundational sphere of the clear light of voidness within

everyone's mind-stream is as all-pervasive as is space.

The Dharmakaya is the body (kaya) that subsumes all things (dharmas) that can be perceived and expressed by a Buddha. It is the knowledge that directly perceives the ultimate nature of the void sphere of all things and is the direct cause for a Buddha's accomplishing unsurpassed benefits for all sentient beings.

The Buddha-nature is voidness or the Dharmakaya from the point of view of its being the inherent potentiality of Buddhahood. It is innate within the mind-stream of all sentient beings. Samantabhadra is the Dharmakaya personified as the primordial Buddha (Adi-Buddha). The mind of Samantabhadra is a synonym for the intentionality of the Buddhas and is the inherent awareness (svasamveda; rang-rig) that fully realizes its own enlightened state. In other words, although primordial awarences of the abiding nature of reality is inherent in the mind-streams of all sentient beings, they are unaware of it. It is shrouuded in ignorance or literally in "unawareness." Samantabhadra. however, is aware of his own enlightened state. When you likewise become aware of your own innate condition, you recover the mind of Samantabhadra. To realize directly this all-pervasive intentionality of the Buddhas, the mind of Samantabhadra, is the supreme view of reality according to Dzogchen. It is based on directly introducing the disciple to the innate Dharmakaya within his own mind-stream.

On the sphere that is perfectly pure there are clouds of fleeting obscurations. These are deceptive appearances, (projected by) the minds of sentient beings. Through these appearances, based on nothing real, the three realms and six classes of beings are perpetuated.

> The void sphere of all things is perfectly pure, free from all mental fabrications. On it, the ignorant mind projects ephemeral taints in the manner of clouds obscuring the sky. When these taints of ignorance or unawareness obscure the sphere of voidness, there appear the abodes of the three realms (desire, form and formless) and the six classes of beings (hell creatures, hungry ghosts, animals, humans, anti-gods and gods). In other words, these taints appear as the realms and beings of samsara, although they have no real existence of their own. These appearances arise from deception and confusion, and because of them sentient beings wander from one physical abode to another, continuously.
>
> The Buddha-nature is the actual nature of Samantabhadra inherent in everyone from time immemorial. It pervades all beings. The mind of Samantabhadra is compared with the sky or space, because it is all-pervasive. Such a mind perceives the void nature of all things and recognizes this as if seeing itself in a mirror. Therefore the mind of Samantabhadra is said "to recognize by itself its own face."
>
> When beings do not recognize themselves in this way, their innate Dharmakaya or Buddha-nature becomes for them an "alaya" or "foundation of everything." At this stage because there is not yet any grasping at a differentiation of objects within that foundation, it is still likened to the sky and is characterized by blissfulness and voidness. In other words, when you fail to see the Dharmakaya as your own nature, that Dharmakaya becomes for you an "alaya"—the

source of everything of both samsara and nirvana. However, it is not yet actively producing these things. It is the potential for this process and thus is undifferentiated.

From the play of that alaya foundation there arises the sort of unawareness or ignorance that causes you to think of yourself as a single, unique individual. This subtle cognition that thinks "I am" is known as self-preoccupation (ahamkara). From it arise the consciousness grasping for "I" and "mine" which thinks to group or draw things to itself in order to establish or prove its own existence. It is through this process that graspable objects arise.

If at this stage you simply let go the arisal of graspable objects—leaving them the moment they arise without pursuing them or trying to prove anything—the process terminates. All that has arisen subsides and dissolves. But if they are not let go, there is the further arisal of specific sensory consciousnesses and the identification that "this consciousness is grasping this object" and "that consciousness is grasping that one." With this ensues the process of naming and giving meaning to those names. This is how grasping formulates.

Thus once the idea of "I" and "mine" has arisen, the entire mechanism of sense objects and consciousness, or subject and object, proceeds in order to gratify the acquisitiveness of this imagined "I" through concrete sensory experiences. The imagined "I" tries to make itself feel real by creating and pursuing sensory experiences. This is a brief description of how grasping consciousness and grasped-at objects arise, producing and perpetuating samsara

Whenever anything appears, no matter what it is, it is non-existent on the ultimate level. Like clouds in the sky, these appearances (come and go) merely because of fleeting circumstances. Therefore samsara is over-estimated. In actual nature, it falls apart.

> Sentient beings grasp as real all objects and moments of consciousness produced through the above process. However, if examined thoroughly, their nature is voidness. Ultimately nothing can be found. Everything of relative reality appears through ever-changing momentary causes like clouds in the sky.
>
> When moisture in the air is moved about by the wind, clouds are formed in the sky. But since clouds are the manifestations of the wind and moisture of the sky, it is impossible to conceive of them as being really different or separate from it. They have no other place to go to establish their existence. Clouds can only gather in the sky and then vanish from it.
>
> In the same way the deceptive appearances generated by your mind's unawareness or ignorance produce the three realms and the six types of beings. The mind is like the moisture, unawareness like the wind, the various realms and deceptive appearances are like the clouds and the sky is the Buddha-nature. The mind, as a cognitive possibility, is inherent in the Buddha-nature in the same way as moisture is inherent in the atmosphere. Driven by the winds of ignorance, the deceptive appearances of samsara gather as clouds. The force that causes the dissolution of these appearances is awareness, that is awareness that none of these appearances are beyond having voidness as their nature. There is no other place for them to be fabricated out of

than from voidness, nor is there any other place for them to go.

To think, therefore, that samsara has true existence is an over-estimation or interpolation. It imagines to exist that which is fact does not. Samsara's three realms are merely an appearance based on nothing real. They are created by the interpolation that "That is this" and "There is that," and subsequently you grasp at your own interpolations. When you realize their actual nature, they naturally disperse like clouds from the sky.

Although not really existent, things still appear. From their own side, however, (such things) are void by nature. These void appearances do not actually exist. They are like a blur of falling hairs (seen by someone with cataract), or like a dream, a mirage or a conchshell perceived as yellow (by someone with jaundice). From time immemorial such appearances have never been (validly) experienced as existing in the manner they appear. They have no foundation, no support, no beginning, middle or end. You must realize that from primordial time everything by nature is pure.

Thus whether samsaric appearances, sentient beings, the environment or whatever—there are no (outer) objects (for consciousness) to grasp. They are like magical creations or visual apparitions. Furthermore, in the exact same manner, there is no (inner) consciousness to grasp anything. All is pure like empty space. As both consciousness and its objects do not really exist, samsara has never been experienced as being existent. By realizing that it is a deceptive appearance and by nature not really existent, you become liberated from it.

When you realize the abiding nature of all things, there is no other course but liberation, namely through the dissolution of the clouds of

> deceptive appearances, leaving you with the void sky of your Buddha-nature.

Things to be abandoned or adopted, causes, effects and circumstances are all appearances. Because they themselves are pure you must realize that the actual nature of reality on the ultimate level is beyond all cause and effect.

> The abiding nature of all things is non-independent existence. If it did not go beyond causality, then ultimately there would have to be two things: (1) the abiding nature, which is non-independent existence, and (2) causality which, having to be different from this nature, would by default have to be truly existent. But since causality is non-truly existent, it cannot be said to be on the same ultimate level as the abiding nature. Therefore the actual nature of reality is beyond cause and effect.

The foundation or support for this (realization) is pure awareness or ultimate bodhichitta.

> When you ascertain the actual abiding nature of all things and arrive at voidness, there is no longer anything that can be labelled or spoken of. Then the objection may arise, "If this is the case, then how can the ultimate be known or realized?" The answer is that at this point there is pure awareness, also known as ultimate bodhichitta or pristine awareness. This is voidness from the point of view of its being realized, taking into consideration that voidness transcends the division into consciousness and an object. Thus it is a way of talking about voidness as if it had a cognitive aspect. To be beyond the division into subject and object does not render voidness as something unrealisable, nor the

> realizer of voidness an inanimate object without any consciousness.

This is the sphere of (natural) nirvana, the great spontaneity, the ultimate level of truth, primordially pure. It has a nature with neither a beginning nor an end. It is clear light by nature—profound, tranquil and free of mental fabrication. It is (pristine awareness) innate within you since time immemorial, the taintless Dharmakaya. It abides as an actuality free from change and transition through the three times (past, present and future). This is the foundational sphere, the vajra essence of reality. Whoever understands it realizes the correct view of the abiding nature of reality. With over- and under-estimation pacified, you understand the essence of ultimate reality.

> To over-estimate reality is to interpolate that it is truly existent, when in fact it is not. Underestimating it is to repudiate or deny its relative existence, for it nevertheless does appear. Therefore the understanding of ultimate and relative realities—the two levels of truth—is a middle path devoid of extremes.
>
> This concludes the discussion of the correct Dzogchen view. Next is how to cultivate that view through meditation.

Stainless meditation is done in a state of comprehending this clear light essence. It is free of mental dullness, agitation and fabrication, has no distraction and is beyond the conventional mind. It is great and extensive, completely pure like the sky. Unrestricted, not imbalanced by selectivity, it is totally beyond all thinking, speaking and conceptualizing.

> In the *Bodhicharyavatara* (IX2), Shantideva writes, "Ultimate reality is not within the range of the conventional mind." Having, in your meditation, gone beyond the relative objects of such a mind, you are in an unrestricted state

transcending the selective process of "This is this" and "That is that." There are no objects to be analyzed or examined and no basis for mental wandering. Afterall, who is the one that is mentally wandering and where are the objects to wander after? You have already arrived at voidness. This meditational state, therefore, is beyond thinking, speaking and conceptualizing because there are no conventional objects to think or speak about on the ultimate level. It is beyond mental dullness as well because the nature of the ultimate is clear light and pristine awareness.

Having completed the topics of the correct view and meditation, what follows is how to act based on that view.

As for activity, whatever appears has no truth and is perfectly pure. Thus whatever internal grasping thoughts arise naturally dissolve.

No matter what thoughts arise during your daily conduct if you recognize their true nature, they have no other course than naturally to subside. In the same way as pictures drawn on water, thoughts that arise do so on the surface of pure awareness and must dissolve again back into that same awareness. But this is not to say that in the process the causes for their arisal simply vanish. Thoughts continue to arise at this stage, but dissolve as soon as they do. They are not pursued.

If there were no further arisal of thought, this state would become the same as the cessation of suffering taught by the Hinayana Sravakas. Without any movement, they achieve a complete cessation. But this is not the Dzogchen method. Instead of trying to bring the conventional thought process to a complete standstill, as a Dzogchen practitioner you learn to recognize the true nature of your thoughts. As soon as they arise you see them for what they are and they naturally subside.

External objects grasped at are like a dream or a mirage. Ultimately neither (consciousness nor objects) are real. Therefore act without either undertaking or rejecting.

Ultimately, nothing to be undertaken or rejected can be established as having true existence. Therefore right action based on the correct view of voidness is beyond the rigid categories of accepting and abandoning.

Whatever arises—either objects or consciousness, defilements, cessations or affirmations—naturally dissolve as soon as it occurs. That is to say, once its true nature is known, it dissolves. And this dissolution is into a state of the Dharmakaya, which has been complete from time immemorial, pervading everything equally. Therefore, having abandoned samsara, there is no need to search for nirvana.

As explained above, when you do not recognize your innate Buddha-nature, then the Dharmakaya becomes for you an alaya foundation. With the subtle cognition of self-preoccupation, this foundation gives rise to thoughts and objects. If you recognize them for what they are and do not indulge yourself in the further processes of differentiation, selectivity and so forth, these thoughts and objects naturally dissolve back into the Dharmakaya awareness of voidness. There is nowhere else for them to go, like clouds dispersing in the sky. It is in this way, then, that you abandon the samsaric cycle of grasping consciousness and grasped-at objects

> without needing to seek a Sravaka's Nirvana of total cessation of conventional thought.

Whatever (objects) appear are like mirrors reflecting the ultimate. Whatever (states of consciousness) arise, naturally dissolve as soon as they are recognized. This is the play of Dharmakaya. Like water and waves, they are one continuum in the Dharmakaya. This is the significance of the ultimate meaning, the very summit of views, the Great Completeness, Dzogchen.

> Whatever objects appear are to be viewed as mirrors, Since their nature is the clear light of voidness, they reflect the ultimate, while their conventional appearance is left unimpeded.
>
> Whatever thoughts arise are to be recognized as coming from voidness and naturally dissolving back into it. They are the play of the Dharmakaya. Like waves and water, never separate from each other, your rising and ebbing thoughts are one continuum with your Dharmakaya.
>
> Thus looking at an object you can see reflected in its voidness your innate Dharamakaya and in its appearance your thoughts—the play of the Dharmakaya.

In short, however you practise, (the most important points are) the natural dissolution of ego-grasping and the purification of delusions in the sphere (of the Dharmakaya). Whoever is skilled in the practice of all these means achieves what is called the removal of confusion while on the path.

By (sailing) the precious great ship of this manner of teaching, may all sentient beings without exception cross the ocean of samsara. On the supreme island of precious, peaceful liberation, may they realize a festival of unending peace and bliss.

4 *Purifying Confusion into Pristine Awareness*

Next is the purification of confusion into pristine awareness. Of the two stages for this, the provisional and ultimate, the first is the provisional. This deals with the time when you are practising on the paths. By familiarizing yourself with profound methods, you will be able to purify whatever delusions arise into their own sphere. To make manifest pristine awareness which is the natural clarity (of the mind) is called purifying confused thoughts into the sphere of pristine awareness.

> The profound methods are those of the outer and inner tantras, more specifically those of the development and completing stages of maha-, anu- and ati-yoga, whereby you come to experience pristine awareness. This awareness of the abiding nature of reality has five aspects, such as mirror-like pristine awareness and so forth. When you are unaware of these aspects, you have confusion. Such a confused or deceived state of mind takes the form of the delusions, such as fearful and angered repulsion. Thus the five major delusions are states of unawareness of the five corresponding types of pristine awareness. If you become aware, the delusions are automatically purified into the sphere of their corresponding pristine awareness and the natural clarity of the mind which had been obscured by confusion is thus made manifest.

This is a brief explanation of the provisional methods. More extensively, these techniques used on the path can be sub-divided as follows.

This can be further divided according to the methods relied upon on the common, special and peerless paths. These are respectively cleansing away (confusing delusions) with their antidotes, transforming them with methods and purifying them into the sphere (of pristine awareness) without abandoning them since they naturally dissolve in their own place. Regardless of how you train yourself with whichever type of purifying (method) you like, the state of cessation and that of purification of the delusions are ultimately the same.

The common path is that of the sutras, as divided into the Hinayana vehicles of the Sravakas and Pratyekabuddhas and the Mahayana one of the Bodhisattvas. On the former you eliminate delusions by abandoning them like poison. On the latter you apply opponent forces such as meditating on love to cleanse away anger, on ugliness for desire, interdependent origination for closed-minded ignorance and so forth.

The special paths are those of the outer and inner tantras whereby delusions are transformed and purified by special methods that take them as a pathway. For instance, on the development stage you cultivate pure vision so that you regard your five aggregate faculties as the heads of the five Buddha-families, your five delusions as the five pristine awarenesss in the form of deities and so forth. On the completing stage you transform delusions by blending them with their corresponding positive attributes through sophisticated techniques involving the energy-systems of the subtle body. Desire is blended with bliss by the practice of psychic heat (*gtum-mo*), anger with the realization of non-true existence by the illusory body practices and closed-minded ignorance with sleep by means of clear light.

The peerless method is that of Dzogchen. By training yourself progressively with the previous techniques you gain the flexibility and experience to be able to master it. You come to realize that confused, deluded thoughts arise and dissolve simultaneously in their own place like drawings on water. Therefore there is no need to abandon delusions. When you realize pristine awareness and the void sphere of all things, they are automatically purified for they naturally dissolve.

Thus since ultimately delusions lack true existence and cannot be found, it does not matter which method you employ to eliminate them. Their cessation and their purification into pristine awareness amount to exactly the same thing. A drawing on water will cease to exist as soon as it is drawn regardless of what method you use to erase it.

When you recognize the natural ground for the arisal of desire, anger, closed-mindedness, pride and jealousy, (you see that) they automatically settle. They naturally dissolve, purified as the five aspects of pristine awareness.

To recognize the natural ground that gives rise to the delusions or, literally, "their own place," means to recognize their actual void nature. Ultimately, deluded thoughts cannot be found. As they arise and subside simultaneously, like drawings on water, they have no truly existent arising, enduring or ceasing as actual events. However, when you are confused about their abiding nature, they seem to be truly real. But, when you recognize them for what they are, you see that they automatically subside and settle without your need to do anything. Like waves automatically settling into water, you cannot actually find that which has been settled and that which has settled it. In this example, the waves are deluded, confused thoughts and the water is the actual nature of the mind itself. Thus when your recognize the nature of the delusions, you see that they have the nature of their corresponding type of pristine awareness. Thus they are purified into these pristine awarenesses and automatically subside.

For example, when you recognize the nature of longing desire with which you single out something pleasing and obsessively long to possess it, you see that this delusion is of the nature of individualizing pristine awareness. In other words, by recognizing the nature of desire, you strip it of your grasping for true existence. In so doing, you make manifest the pristine awareness that had merely individualized or singled out this object. Thus desire has been purified into individualizing pristine awareness.

It is not that at one moment there is a delusion and then, having ceased, there is pristine awareness in the next. Confused, deluded thoughts arise and subside in the same moment. When you are aware of their nature, you have pristine awareness and when unaware, delusion. If you are confused about their nature, you are deluded; if not, they are pure.

Furthermore, it is not that you recognize the nature of the delusions in one moment and then in the next they dissolve into pristine awareness. For instance, it is not that the darkness of

> night first disappears and then you have the light of day. If that were the case, there would be no need for the sun since the darkness would have already disappeared before it rose. Therefore just as the appearance of light is equivalent to the disappearance of darkness, likewise simultaneous is the manifestation of pristine awareness and dissolution of confusion. The only difference between the two is whether or not they are purified in the void sphere of all things. Pristine awareness obscured by the darkness of grasping for true existence is the confusion of the delusions. The delusions purified of such grasping are the pristine awareness.

This is known as the provisional purification of the confusion of the five poisons into the major pristine awarenesses, namely analytic, mirror-like, sphere of voidness, equalizing and accomplishing.

> Desire is being attached to something you consider pleasant. It pervades all the other delusions. For instance, the desire of anger or of fearful and angered repulsion is the wish to be free of something unpleasant, while that of closed-mindedness is the desire to remain unaware of or uninvolved with something. The purification of such fixation on an object is analytic or individualizing pristine awareness. It merely singles out an individual object, without mixing it with anything else, and understands its void nature as non-truly existent.
>
> Fearful and angered repulsion is directed at what you consider unpleasant. Such rejection is purified as mirror-like pristine awareness which merely reflects the object clearly. This type of awareness is defined as that with which clarity is not obstructed, in other words that which can

clearly reflect objects with no obstruction. Its main feature is clarity.

Closed-minded ignorance is a state of darkness in which you do not see anything clearly and have no understanding. Like desire, it too pervades all delusions. Purified, it is the pristine awareness of the void sphere of all things, characterized by a bare non-conceptual understanding of voidness.

Some masters explain these last two correspondences oppositely, namely that purified anger is the sphere of voidness pristine awareness and purified closed-mindedness is the mirror-like one. There is no contradiction in this since each variety of pristine awareness can be subdivided into aspects of each of the five. There are individualizing, mirror-like, sphere of voidness, equalizing and accomplishing aspects of sphere of voidness pristine awareness and so forth. Thus all five types are complete in each one. It is not that they are mutually exclusive entities.

Pride is feeling better than others in terms of social position, family, wealth, intelligence and so on. Equalizing pristine awareness is that which is without such confused discriminations as superior and inferior, good and bad, foreign and native. Thus in the awareness that makes no dualistic discriminations, there is no ground for pride to arise. Therefore the former is the purification of the latter.

Finally, accomplishing pristine awareness is that which offers no hindrance to actions being accomplished effortlessly and spontaneously. It is the purification of jealousy with which you wish someone else had not accomplished something, but you had.

These then are the provisional techniques for purifying confusion into pristine awareness while on the paths to enlightenment. Next is the ultimate purification, namely that of Buddhahood.

As for the ultimate (attainment), when you remove the fleeting stains from the expanse (of the Buddha-nature) and discover the peaceful spotless state of perfection, the nature of this sphere becomes manifest just as it is. The three Buddha Bodies, Dharmakaya, single taste or pristine awareness that you discover is known as the Body of the Sphere (of Voidness) possessing double purity. This is not an object (known) by anyone other than the Buddhas.

The void expanse of the Buddha-nature is naturally pure and pervades all Buddhas and sentient beings, although for the latter it is obscured by the fleeting stains of their ignorance. When you fully see the voidness of these simultaneously arising and dissolving obstacles that have been preventing your liberation and omniscience, and in this way realize your Buddha-nature, this nature acquires a second purity in addition to its natural one. This is the purity of being free of stains. These two purities are like those of polished gold, which is naturally pure and doubly so when all tarnish is removed.

This state of a fully realized Buddha-nature is known as the Body of the Sphere of Voidness possessing double purity and is synonymous with the enlightened state of a Buuddha. Viewed from different aspects, it is either the three Buddha Bodies, the Dharmakaya, the single taste or simply pristine awareness. One of the significances of the term "Dzogchen" or "Great Completeness" is that in the perfect state of Buddhahood all three Buddha Bodies are spontaneously complete. The Dharmakaya fulfilling your own purposes and the two Form Bodies fulfilling those of others do not impede each other, but rather are of one taste. They are simultaneous, spontaneous, inseparable and complete in the sphere of pristine awareness.

The three Buddha Bodies, namely the Body that Subsumes Everything (Dharmakaya), the Utility Body (Sambhogakaya) and Emanation Body (Nirmanakaya), together with pristine awareness, are all incorporated into the Body of the Essential Nature (Svabhavakaya), which is permanent, all-pervasive, unconditioned and without movement or change. Abiding in the sphere of the Dharmakaya, which is a wish-fulfilling gem, the Body of the Virtuous Conduct of Pristine Awareness sports from this state as the Utility and Emanation Bodies which appear respectively to those on the Bodhisattva stages and to other sentient beings. However, they only appear that way through the conjunction of the force of the Buddha's virtuous conduct which, as long as samsara endures, continues unbrokenly to fulfill the wishes (of all sentient beings) like a wish-granting tree or gem, is known as the (ultimate) purification of confusion into pristine awareness.

The Body of the Essential Nature is the abiding nature of all reality, fully pervading and incorporating all Buddha Bodies, being in fact their inseparability. Its cognitive aspect is the Body of Pristine Awareness, the spontaneous play of which is the Buddhas' virtuous conduct that fulfills the wishes of all sentient beings by manifesting Bodies of Form in the same way as the sun emits light.

These Form Bodies are of two types, Utility and Emanation Bodies. The former appear only to Bodhisattvas who have had bare perception of voidness and are thus on one of the ten

> Bodhisattva stages (bhumi). The latter appear to ordinary sentient beings who have accumulated the merit and purity of mind to see them. Thus in the same way that reflections of the moon appear on jewelled surfaces through the combined force of the rays of moonlight and the polish of the jewels, similarly Form Bodies appear in the void space of the Dharmakaya through the combined force of the Buddhas' waves of inspiration and sentient beings' merit. The attainment of their virtuous conduct is the ultimate purification of confusion into pristine awareness.

May the seven-horse-drawn sun, which is the essence of the profound meaning (explained) like this, shed thousands of light-rays of its various words and their meanings on the world of disciples through the pathway of the sky of their minds and thus eliminate the darkness of ignorance from all beings.

Author's Colophon

This joyous festival of the methods (of these teachings), which has been spread for the sake of both myself and others from the excellent house of broad intelligence and enriched with a wealth of hearing, thinking and meditating, has been arranged in accordance with the meaning of the sutras, tantras and essential oral teachings. By the virtue of this, may I and all sentient beings level the mountain of samsara in this lifetime and attain to the supreme peaceful and spotless state of enlightenment. May we become Buddhas and completely accomplish the aims of ourselves and others. And then in a land adorned with expansive snow-mountains of clear meaning, may the sun of our white virtuous qualities, which extends to the limit of all directions, highlight points on the treasure-field of the scriptures, thereby bringing joy to the masses of beings with faith.

This work, called "The Four-Themed Precious Garland" has been completely by the yogi of the Supreme Vehicle, Kunkhyen Ngazi Wangpo (kuun-mkhyen ngag-gi dbango, klong-chen rab-'byams-pa, 1308-1363) in one sitting by the light of the waxing crystal moon in the excellent house of Samantabhadra within the grove called "A Cloud of Flowers" on the slopes of Limestone Mountain. May a rain of great bliss fall for all times and in all directions as in the Golden Age, fulfilling all the hopes and wishes made by everyone.

Notes

1. The Form Body having five certainties refers to the Utility Body (Sambhogakaya) of a Buddha, which always. (1) has the 112 bodily marks of a Buddha, (2) resides in pure-land Buddha-fields (3) until the end of samsara (4) teaching the Mahayana Dharma (5) to Arya Bodhisattvas.
2. According to the Abhidharma teachings, the universe goes through cycles of creation and destruction. At various intervals it is destroyed by the elements of fire, water wind.
3. The three faults refer to the sufferings of misery, change and extensiveness. The first is that of obvious pain such as from sickness and so forth. The suffering of change comes about, for instance, when you are cold and stand in the sun, only to become too hot and uncomfortable and then must go into the shade again. The suffering of extensiveness comes from being born with contaminated aggregate physical and mental faculties which, by their very nature, attract like a magnet sickness, old age and other such sufferings.

   These three faults can be expanded into a list of eight. These are the sufferings of birth, old age, sickness, death, being parted from what you like, meeting with what you do not like, not obtaining the things you like even though you try to find them and having contaminated aggregates, received according to your past karma and defilements, which are of the very nature of suffering.
4. The eight worldly feelings are being pleased when receiving gifts, love, attention and so forth, and displeased when not, being elated when everything is going well and depressed when it is not, being happy when hearing pleasantries and unhappy when not, and being self-satisfied when praised or complimented and annoyed when abused or degraded.
5. The four immeasurables are equanimity, love, compassion

and joy. These are the prayer and wishes that all sentient beings be unbiased, endowed with happiness, free from suffering and never parted from joy.

6. The paths and facets are common to both the Hinayana and Mahayana traditions. If you practice with the motivation of the former tradition, they bring you the perfection of liberation as either as shravaka or pratyekabuddha arhat, but if with a Mahayana motivation, the perfection of Enlightenment as a Buddha.

In general, on the path of accumulation you achieve mental quiescence (shamatha) and a presumptive understanding of voidness from the power of hearing a correct explanation of it. On the path of preparation you attain penetrative insight (vipashyana) and a conceptual, inferential understanding of voidness. With the attainment of non-conceptual, bare perception of Voidness in your meditation sessions, you reach the path of seeing and become an Arya or Noble One. If you are travelling these paths as a Bodhisattva with the enlightened motive of bodhichitta, this is also the attainment of the first Bodhisattva stage. On the path of meditation you familiarize yourself with such bare perception in order to eliminate the obstacles preventing awareness of your Buddha-nature at all times and pass through the second to the tenth Bodhisattva stages. On the final path of no more learning, you fully realize at all times the Void sphere of all things, your Buddha-nature, the pristine awareness of the inseparability of Voidness and appearance. This is the attainment of the Full Enlightenment of Buddhahood.

The thirty-seven facets which bring about this attainment or that of a Hinayana Arhat are the four close contemplations, the four states of pure abandonment, the four legs of extra-physical powers, the five powers, five forces, seven limbs bringing perfection and the eight noble paths of the Aryas. The first three sets are mastered on the path of accumulation, the five powers and forces on that of preparation, the seven limbs on that of seeing and the eight noble paths on the path of meditation.

The four close contemplations are (1) of the body, in order to understand it as an example of the noble truth of suffering, particularly in terms of the suffering of extensiveness, (2) of the feelings, in order to see them as the noble truth of the cause of suffering—the cause of suffering is grasping: happiness is grasping not be separated from pleasure, unhappiness is grasping to be parted from pain and indifference is the desire not to change, (3) of the mind, in order to see its ultimate nature as an example of the noble truth of cessation of suffering, and (4) of all things, in order to understand what is to be abandoned and adopted, in other words, the noble truth of the path.

The four states of abandonment are paths for fortifying your abandonment of non-virtue and adoption of virtue. They are meditation on (1) cultivating virtuous actions and qualities that you have not yet developed, (2) enhancing those you have already developed, (3) stopping the further increase of your non-virtues and (4) keeping yourself from developing non-virtuous qualities that you have not yet acquired.

The four legs of extra-physical powers are states of single-minded concentration gained from mental quiescence and are for achieving the power of being able to multiply and contract your physical form at will in order to benefit yourself and others. These legs are those of (1) intention to achieve such an advanced attainment of mental quiescence, (2) enthusiastic perseverance for it, (3) contemplation on the methods for achieving it and (4) discrimination on how to use it. They are attained on the third of the nine subdivisions of the path of accumulation.

The second of the five paths, that of preparation, is divided into four stages: heat, peak, patience and supreme Dharma. The five powers bring your achievement of the first two and prepare you for attaining the latter two. They are states of mind directed at the four noble truths, allowing you to gain a deeper realization of them. The five are (1) the power of faith or full belief in these truths, (2) that of enthusiastic perseverance for their realization, (3) mindfulness of them, (4) single-minded concentration on them and (5) that of discriminating awareness of their individual aspects. The five forces are the same as the powers and are also directed at the four noble truths. They are stronger, however, than the former set and cannot be overcome by their opponents of disbelief, laziness, forgetfulness, distraction and decreasing wisdom. Attained on the patience stage, they bring about achievement of bare perception of voidness on the path of seeing.

The seven limbs bringing perfection are achieved on this third path, that of seeing. Also directed at the four noble truths, they are wisdoms of Arya beings that eliminate those delusions obscuring your Buddha-nature that are abandoned on this particular path. They are (1) pure mindfulness, (2) discrimination, (3) enthusiastic perseverance, (4) joy, (5) flexibility, (6) single-minded concentration and (7) equanimity. Because these limbs are based on the bare perception of voidness, they see the four noble truths more clearly than before and are able to eliminate more delusions.

The final delusions obscuring your Buddha-nature are abandoned on the path of meditation. They are eliminated by the eight noble paths of the Aryas, which are right (1) view, (2) aspiration, (3) speech, (4) action, (5) livelihood, (6) effort, (7) mindfulness and (8) single-minded concentration, all directed at the four noble truths. It is in this progressive manner, then, that mastery of these thirty-seven facets of practice as a Bodhisattva brings you the Full Enlightenment of a Buddha, as explained in the "Abhisamayalamkara" by Maitreya.

7. The sixteen types of voidness are divided according to the different bases for the imputation of voidness, that is the various types of phenomena that lack true inherent existence. These are the voidness of (1) internal phenomena, (2) external ones, (3) those that are both internal and external, (4) voidness, (5) greatness, namely of everything in the ten directions, (6) ultimacy, namely of nirvana and of the noble truth of cessation, (7) conditioned phenomena, (8) unconditioned phenomena, (9) that which is beyond extremes, namely interdependent origination, (10) that which is beginningless and endless, namely samsara or cyclic existence, (11) that which cannot be abandoned, namely the stages of the Mahayana path, (12) the nature of things, (13) everything, (14) definitions, (15) that which cannot be objectified, namely past, present and future, and (16) that which is not a phenomenon,

namely the non-true existence of everything. From the point of view of voidness, however, these sixteen are all the same.

8. The six perfection are of generosity, moral discipline, patience, enthusiastic perseverance, meditative concentration and discriminatory awareness or wisdom.
9. Cf. bDud-'joms Rinpoche 'Jigs-bral ye-shes rdo-rje, ``gSang-sngags snga-'gyur rnying-ma-ba'i bstan-pa'i rnam-bzhag mdo-tzam brjod-pa legs-bshad snang-ba'i dga'-ston" (Kalimpong ed.) 41B-45A.